EARTH'S
NATURAL
BIOMES

FRESHWATER BIOMES

Louise and Richard Spilsbury

Crabtree Publishing Company
www.crabtreebooks.com

Crabtree Publishing Company
www.crabtreebooks.com
1-800-387-7650

Published in Canada
Crabtree Publishing
616 Welland Avenue
St. Catharines, ON
L2M 5V6

Published in the United States
Crabtree Publishing
PMB 59051
350 Fifth Ave, 59th Floor
New York, NY 10118

Published in 2018 by CRABTREE PUBLISHING COMPANY.

First published in 2017 by Wayland
Copyright © Wayland, 2017

Authors: Louise Spilsbury, Richard Spilsbury

Editors: Hayley Fairhead, Philip Gebhardt

Design: Smart Design Studio

Map (page 6) by Stefan Chabluk

Editorial director: Kathy Middleton

Proofreader: Lorna Notsch

Prepress technician: Tammy McGarr

Print and production coordinator: Margaret Amy Salter

Photographs

All photographs except where mentioned supplied by
Nature Picture Library www.naturepl.com

Front cover(main), p16 and p30 Alex Mustard; title page(main)
and p14 Klein and Hubert; p4 Kirkendall-Spring; p5, title page(b)
and p31(t) Tony Heald; p6 Jerry Monkman; p7 Anup Shah; p8,
front cover(tr) and p31(b) Wild Wonders of Europe / Radisics;
p9(main) and title page(b) Doug Perrine; p9(inset) Jurgen Freund;
p10 and front cover(br) Christophe Courteau; p11 Linda Pitkin /
2020 VISION; p12 and contents(b) Alex Hyde; p13 and title page(t)
Michael Loup; p15(main) and back cover(l) Michael Loup; p15(inset)
and front cover(tl) Thomas Lazar; p17 Tim Laman; p18(main and
inset) Bernard Castelein; p19 Anup Shah; p20 Chris Mattison; p21
Bence Mate; p23 Juan Manuel Borrero; p26 and contents(t) Tim
Laman; p27 and imprint page(t) Eric Baccega; p28 Franco Barnfi.

Photographs supplied by Shutterstock: p23 Chung Toan Co; p24
Deyan Georgiev; p25 Flaxphotos; p29 theskaman306.

Printed in the USA/122019/BG20171102

Library and Archives Canada Cataloguing in Publication

Spilsbury, Louise, author
    Freshwater biomes / Louise Spilsbury, Richard Spilsbury.

(Earth's natural biomes)
Includes index.
Issued in print and electronic formats.
ISBN 978-0-7787-3994-4 (hardcover).--
ISBN 978-0-7787-4047-6 (softcover).--
ISBN 978-1-4271-2004-5 (HTML)

    1. Freshwater ecology--Juvenile literature. 2. Fresh water--
Juvenile literature. I. Spilsbury, Richard, 1963-, author II. Title.

QH541.5.F7S67 2018   j577.6   C2017-906889-X
                                            C2017-906890-3

Library of Congress Cataloging-in Publication Data

Names: Spilsbury, Louise, author. | Spilsbury, Richard, 1963- author.
Title: Freshwater biomes / Louise Spilsbury, Richard Spilsbury.
Description: New York, New York : Crabtree Publishing Company,
    2018. | Series: Earth's natural biomes | Includes index. |
Identifiers: LCCN 2017051156 (print) | LCCN 2017054839 (ebook) |
    ISBN 9781427120045 (Electronic HTML) |
    ISBN 9780778739944 (reinforced library binding) |
    ISBN 9780778740476 (pbk.)
Subjects: LCSH: Freshwater ecology--Juvenile literature. | Freshwater
    habitats--Juvenile literature. | Freshwater biodiversity
    conservation--Juvenile literature.
Classification: LCC QH541.5.F7 (ebook) | LCC QH541.5.F7 S685
    2018 (print) | DDC 577.6--dc23
LC record available at https://lccn.loc.gov/2017051156

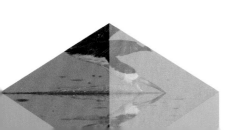

CONTENTS

WHAT ARE FRESHWATER BIOMES?

From rushing rivers to calm lakes and soggy marshes, freshwater biomes are some of the most varied in the world. Freshwater biomes have one main thing in common: they usually contain water with less than one percent salt, compared to seawater, which is 3.5 percent salt.

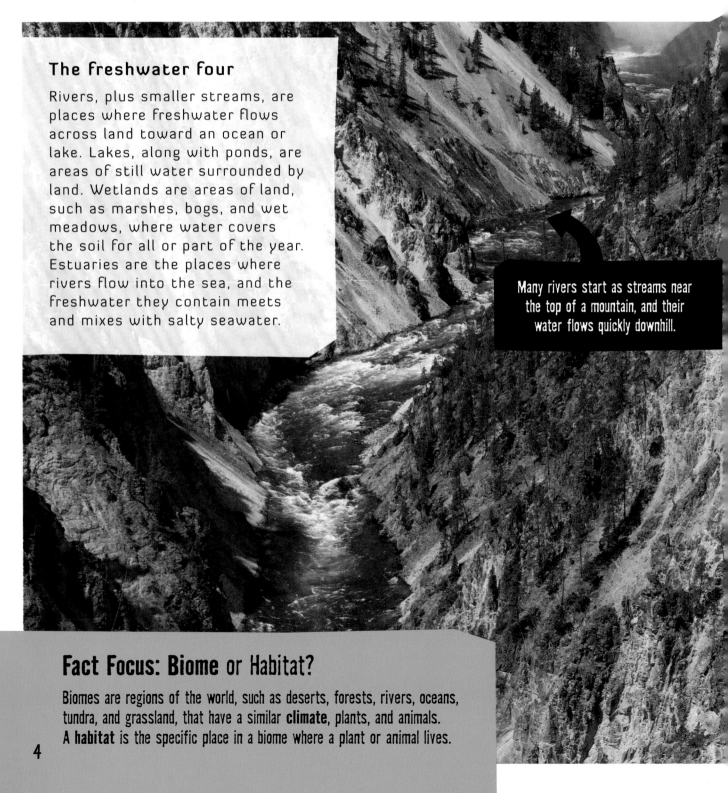

The freshwater four

Rivers, plus smaller streams, are places where freshwater flows across land toward an ocean or lake. Lakes, along with ponds, are areas of still water surrounded by land. Wetlands are areas of land, such as marshes, bogs, and wet meadows, where water covers the soil for all or part of the year. Estuaries are the places where rivers flow into the sea, and the freshwater they contain meets and mixes with salty seawater.

Many rivers start as streams near the top of a mountain, and their water flows quickly downhill.

Fact Focus: Biome or Habitat?

Biomes are regions of the world, such as deserts, forests, rivers, oceans, tundra, and grassland, that have a similar **climate**, plants, and animals. **A habitat** is the specific place in a biome where a plant or animal lives.

Freshwater life

A whole range of living things has **adapted** to life in freshwater biomes. Trees, reeds, irises, and other plants grow in the damp soil at the water's edge. Some plants, such as water lilies, live in the water. Freshwater animals, such as tiny water fleas, snails, and fish, live underwater. Other animals, including enormous crocodiles and anaconda snakes, visit the water to feed.

Vital resource

Freshwater plants and animals have an advantage over those living on dry land, because they usually have a constant supply of water. Living things are made up mostly of water, and they need to constantly replenish this water to survive.

Skimmers fly low over freshwater lakes, plowing their large beaks through the water as they go. Their beaks snap shut to trap any fish they scoop up.

Amazing Adaptation

Adaptations are special features or body parts that living things use to help them survive in a biome. Diving beetles store air bubbles under their wing cases while they are at a lake's surface. They use the air bubbles as an air supply when they hunt underwater.

FRESHWATER AROUND THE WORLD

Only about three percent of Earth's total water is freshwater, and much of this is frozen at the North and South **Poles**. The rest is found in freshwater biomes around the world.

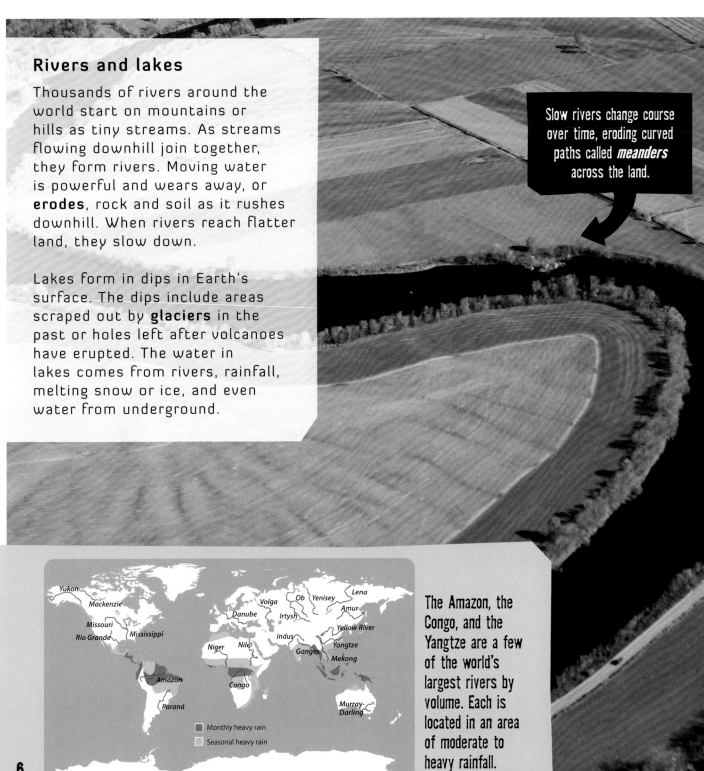

Rivers and lakes

Thousands of rivers around the world start on mountains or hills as tiny streams. As streams flowing downhill join together, they form rivers. Moving water is powerful and wears away, or **erodes**, rock and soil as it rushes downhill. When rivers reach flatter land, they slow down.

Lakes form in dips in Earth's surface. The dips include areas scraped out by **glaciers** in the past or holes left after volcanoes have erupted. The water in lakes comes from rivers, rainfall, melting snow or ice, and even water from underground.

Slow rivers change course over time, eroding curved paths called *meanders* across the land.

Yukon
Mackenzie
Missouri
Mississippi
Rio Grande
Niger
Nile
Danube
Volga
Irtysh
Ob
Yenisey
Lena
Amur
Indus
Ganges
Yellow River
Yangtze
Mekong
Amazon
Congo
Paraná
Murray-Darling

Monthly heavy rain
Seasonal heavy rain

The Amazon, the Congo, and the Yangtze are a few of the world's largest rivers by volume. Each is located in an area of moderate to heavy rainfall.

Wetlands and estuaries

Wetlands are damp areas of land that form where river, lake, or spring water soaks flat areas of soil. Wetlands usually get wetter after rainy periods, but some can dry up in drier spells of weather.

In estuaries, water levels rise when tides carry seawater inland twice a day. This makes the freshwater in the rivers salty. At low tide, the water level drops and the water becomes less salty again. Plants and animals living in these areas are adapted to deal with the changes in the water levels and saltiness.

A range of animals, including proboscis monkeys, probe estuary mud for **prey**, such as crabs, in Borneo in Southeast Asia.

Fact Focus: The Water Cycle

Freshwater biomes depend on the water cycle. This is the continual process of water moving from the land into the **atmosphere** and back again. Water **evaporates** from the surface of freshwater biomes. Later, it **condenses** into droplets of water that form clouds. When it rains, water falls back to Earth and refills sources of freshwater.

FRESHWATER PLANTS

Plants are a vital part of freshwater biomes. Different plants are adapted to grow in different types of freshwater environments.

Water-lily leaves have a large **surface area** and air-filled spaces to keep them afloat. They can even support the weight of nesting birds, such as this tern.

Powerful waters

River plants have to cope with moving water. Plants, such as eelgrass, have long thin leaves and tough roots so they don't get washed away. Water flows around the leaves rather than pushing against and damaging them. Ferns and mosses grow on rocks next to streams, gaining a supply of water from the spray.

Still, deep water

Many lake plants, such as irises, grow at the water's edge. In deeper water, toward the middle, there is less light for **photosynthesis**. This is the process during which green plants use the sun's energy to make sugars for their food from carbon dioxide in the air and water. Many lake plants have leaves that float. Some, such as water lilies, are rooted to the lake floor, but others, including duckweed, have no stems, just leaves with **roots** dangling in the water.

Low oxygen

Most living things need **oxygen** to survive. Wetlands are saturated with water either permanently or seasonally. However, they are short on oxygen because air containing oxygen does not mix into the still water and spaces in the soil are waterlogged. Plants called cattails get around this by taking in air through their leaves and storing it in chambers in their stems for the roots to use.

Harmful salt

Most plants can be harmed or killed by large amounts of salt. Estuary plants take in saltwater through their roots, but get rid of excess amounts that could be damaging. For example, glasswort and samphire plants store freshwater from rivers in pouches, called bladders, in their leaves to **dilute** the saltwater.

Amazing Adaptation

Mangrove leaves contain spaces called glands. Salt from the sap of the plant collects in the glands. The leaves often appear white because of the salt crystals that form on them after the plant expels salty water from the glands.

Aerial roots on mangrove plants act as supports to hold their tops above water when the tide is in. Holes on the central stem take in air for the roots.

RIVER LIFE

River animals cope with the demands of life in moving water using a host of different adaptations.

Giant otters build dens in riverbanks, but spend much of their days in the water hunting prey, including eels, anacondas, and alligator–like animals called caimans.

Giant otters

Giant otters from South America are the longest of all otters, reaching 6 feet (1.8 m) long. Like other otters, they have powerful, broad tails and **webbed feet** to steer and push fast through the water. They have **dense** fur that repels water, so their skin doesn't get too wet and cold, and nostrils and ears that close tight when they swim.

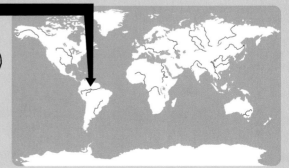

Fact File: Amazon River

Location: South America
Size: 4,010 mi. (6,400 km)/2,700,000 sq. mi. (7,000,000 km²) drainage basin
Overview: The second longest river in the world after the Nile, but the one with most water in it. The Amazon has 2,500 types of fish, including electric eels and piranhas, plus pink river dolphins and giant otters.

Armored crayfish

Like crabs and lobsters, crayfish have a tough, hard **exoskeleton**. This is like a suit of armor that protects their soft bodies from attack by **predators**. It also protects them if fast-moving river water bashes them against a rock.

Exoskeletons do not stretch as crayfish grow. Several times a year, a crayfish sheds its old exoskeleton when it is feeling tight and makes a new, bigger exoskeleton from **calcium** stored in its stomach.

By day, crayfish hide under sunken logs and rocks. At night, they come out to feed on riverbeds, grasping food, such as worms and leaves, in their tough claws.

Crayfish eyes grow on stalks and can move independently to spot prey. Their long **antennae** also help them feel and taste prey in water that is sometimes murky.

Amazing Adaptation

Crayfish have spikes on their large legs that help them to grip onto wet, slippery rocks to stop moving water from washing them off while they feed.

LAKE LIFE

Many animals that live in lakes and ponds are deadly predators that have clever ways to make sure they catch their prey on or in the still waters.

Hairy legs

In parts of Europe, raft spiders sit at pond edges or on floating plants, with their legs resting on the water's surface. They can feel the tiny ripples of the water made by prey, such as water insects or even tadpoles as they swim upward. Then a raft spider races over the surface of the water to catch its prey.

The raft spider's legs have a waxy surface that repels water. In addition, water forms a kind of skin at its surface known as **surface tension**. The spider's light weight and large surface area prevent it breaking through the surface of the water. This allows it to walk on water.

Raft spiders have a body measuring 0.87 inches (22 mm) long and a leg span of 2.8 inches (70 mm). They can run across water to catch prey and even continue the chase underwater by sprinting along submerged plants!

Killer fish

Pike are deadly lake predators with large eyes for spotting prey, such as newts, crayfish, fish (including smaller pike), and ducklings. The pike's green, speckled skin helps it to hide among plants in a lake, so that its prey doesn't see this deadly predator until it's too late.

Pike strike quickly. They have long, thin **streamlined** bodies that are designed to slip through the water easily. As a pike darts after its prey, its mouth opens to snatch its victim in its sharp teeth. The teeth also curve backward so that once a pike catches slippery prey in its large mouth, its victim cannot escape, however much it struggles.

A pike lurks among lake plants until prey gets near and then it shoots quickly forward by beating its strong tail **fins**.

Fact File: Lake Baikal

Location: Russia, Central Asia
Size: 12,150 sq. mi. (31,500 km²)
Overview: The biggest lake (by volume) in the world, Baikal contains 20 percent of the world's freshwater! It is home to several animals found nowhere else, including freshwater sponges, oil fish, and Baikal seals.

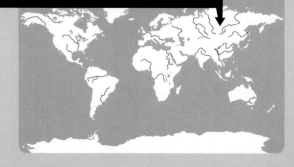

WETLAND LIFE

The muddy areas of shallow water in wetlands make ideal stopping-off points for birds to rest, feed, and drink during long trips between summer and winter feeding grounds. Other animals, from hippos to beavers, are perfectly adapted to wetland life.

Happy hippos

A hippopotamus is a huge, barrel-shaped animal with thin skin that loses moisture easily in hot, dry air. A hippo keeps its skin wet by spending up to 16 hours a day lazing in shallow water. Its ears, eyes, and nostrils are on the top of its head so that while its body is underwater it can still breathe and keep a lookout out for predators, such as crocodiles.

Hippos are very heavy, with bodies so dense they can sink to the bottom and push off from the mud to walk along underwater. They can hold their breath for five minutes.

Hippos feed on wetland grasses and use wetland mud and water to keep cool in the hot African sun.

Fact File: Okavango delta

Location: Botswana, Africa
Size: 2,300–3,100 sq. mi. (6,000–8,000 km^2) in the dry season to 6,000 sq. mi. (15,580 km^2) in the wet season
Overview: A famous wetland on the Okavango River. It is home to a wide range of animals, including dragonflies, storks, and hippos.

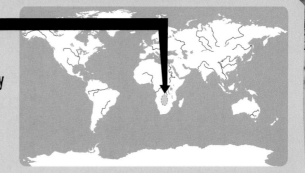

Wetland builder

Beavers are **rodents** with big, sharp teeth they use like chisels to cut down trees! They pile logs and branches with mud and stones to make **dams** that block streams and cause flooding in **valleys**. Beavers build homes, called lodges, in the deep ponds created in the valleys.

Lodges are protected spaces where beavers rest, keep warm during winter, and have their young. Beavers swim in and out of their lodge through underwater entrances hidden out of sight from predators on land. The wetlands that beavers build are important habitats for other animals, such as frogs and ducks.

Amazing Adaptation

A beaver's feet are webbed between the toes. Its back feet are bigger than its front feet. These wide, flat feet, along with its paddle-shaped tail, help the beaver swim.

Beavers live in North America and northern Europe. They can chew through a 5-inch (12-cm) willow tree in three minutes! They eat the bark and leaves, as well as use the branches and trunks as building materials.

ESTUARY LIFE

Estuaries and the marshy areas around them, called salt marshes, provide shelter for many different animals. Some of them have amazing ways of coping with the daily changes in this biome.

Safe haven

Salt marshes and mangrove forests have calm, shallow water and the mud is rich in **nutrients**. Mangrove and other plant roots provide a safe haven where young fish, crabs, snails, and other animals can feed and grow up safely. The waters are home to animals, such as manatees and turtles, that graze on the estuary grasses and come to the surface to breathe.

Manatees, which live in estuaries in the Caribbean Sea and the Gulf of Mexico, use their huge lips to grasp, pluck, and move grasses into their mouth. Their teeth are designed for chewing only. When they wear down, new ones grow.

Amazing Adaptation

Some estuary **bacteria** use **sulfate** found in the mud to release energy from their food. Estuaries can smell bad because this process releases a gas that smells like rotten eggs!

Walking fish

Mudskippers are fish that can walk, climb, or skip across land. They leave estuary waters to hunt prey and to find other areas of water or other mudskippers to **breed** with. When they are underwater, mudskippers breathe using body parts called **gills** that take in oxygen from the water, as most fish do. Before leaving the water, they fill pouches around the gills with water and use these like oxygen tanks to allow them to breathe on dry land. To keep their skin wet out of water, they often roll in muddy puddles.

Amazing Adaptation

When mudskippers are on land, they can use their front fins like legs to walk around!

Mudskippers spend more time on land than underwater along the coastal estuaries of the Pacific and Indian Oceans. They feed mostly on small fish, worms, and insects in the mud.

BORN SURVIVORS

Some animals have amazing ways to make sure their young get the best start in life in freshwater biomes.

From egg to adult

In ponds and lakes, some fish lay eggs that float on the surface. In rivers, some fish stick their eggs to plants or stones to stop them from being washed away. Dragonflies are insects that also start life as an egg underwater.

Female dragonflies attach their eggs to underwater plants in ponds or marshes. The **nymphs** that hatch have gills and hunt small prey. As a nymph eats and grows, its skin becomes tight and splits open, revealing a new, larger skin. After one to two years underwater, the nymph climbs up a plant onto the riverbank. Its skin splits one last time, and a dragonfly with beautiful wings emerges.

Amazing Adaptation

Dragonflies have four wings and can twist, turn, and fly upside down above water to catch insects.

The adult dragonfly in the large image emerged from the nymph skin it had outgrown (see empty skin in inset picture). It only lives for about two months as a flying adult.

Caring crocodiles

Crocodiles and alligators may be very fierce, but the females are gentle, caring mothers. Each makes a nest of mud and plants on the banks of warm rivers. The reptile then lays her eggs inside the nest and stays nearby for up to three months. She watches over her eggs to make sure they don't get washed away and nothing eats them.

When the baby crocodiles are ready to hatch, they call out from inside the eggs. Once they have hatched, their mother helps them dig themselves out of the nest, and then she carefully scoops them up into her huge mouth and carries them to the water. She continues to watch over the youngsters for up to two years, while they learn to feed and fend for themselves.

Even though this Nile crocodile mother has very sharp teeth and crushing jaws, she can carry up to 15 babies in her mouth at a time without hurting them!

EAT OR BE EATEN

Every living thing needs energy to survive. When a freshwater animal eats a plant or another animal, some of that energy is transferred to the predator. A **food chain** shows who eats whom and, therefore, who receives the energy.

The first link in the chain

All food chains begin with plants, and a major energy source for plants is sunlight. Freshwater plants, from tiny algae to mighty swamp cypresses, use photosynthesis in leaves to convert that energy into sugars. They use the sugars to live and grow. Some plants, such as irises and water lotuses, store sugars as **starch** in roots and other parts for future use.

Amazing Adaptation

Some plants, such as the Venus flytrap, that live in boggy wetlands get few nutrients from the soil they grow in. They trap and **digest** insects to supplement their diets.

When a wasp lands on a Venus flytrap's leaf, the leaf snaps shut. Spikes along the leaf's edges form a cage from which the insect cannot escape!

Freshwater chains

Plant eaters in freshwater biomes gain energy when they eat plant parts and the sugar and starches stored within them. Plant eaters range from tiny snails to hippos.

Animals that eat freshwater plant eaters range from birds to crocodiles. Some animals in freshwater food chains live in the water all the time, but others, like raccoons that eat crabs, visit just to feed.

The fish this egret has caught to eat contains energy. This comes from what the fish has eaten, including plant-like algae and snails, which graze on freshwater plants.

Last links in the chain

When dead plants and animals sink to the bottom of a freshwater biome, animals, such as flatworms and crayfish, feed on them. Bacteria in the water and mud break down, or **decompose**, the bits they leave behind. This returns some nutrients from the remains to the biome for new plants and algae to use for their growth, maintaining the food chain cycle.

Fact Focus: Food Webs

A **food web** shows how living things can be connected by different food chains. For example, shrimp and freshwater mollusks eat plankton. Small fish eat freshwater mollusks. Salmon eat small fish, freshwater mollusks, and shrimp.

21

PEOPLE AND FRESHWATER BIOMES

Many people live on or near freshwater biomes and use them as a source of water. But rivers and lakes are also a source of food and a transport route for boats. In some cases, water provides a living space.

Floating lives

Some people live at the edge of rivers, on land that can flood when water levels rise during wet seasons. So they may live in houses on stilts. Other people use freshwater biomes as workplaces. For example, in parts of Thailand and Vietnam people sell fruit, vegetables, and other goods at floating markets. There are even groups of people who live on the surface of freshwater biomes. The Uros people on Lake Titicaca, in Peru, live in communities on giant floating islands made of reeds.

New reeds are added each year to the floating islands on Lake Titicaca to replace reeds that have rotted in the water.

Cities by the water

Many major cities worldwide are situated by freshwater biomes. New Orleans, Louisiana, on the Mississippi River is just one example. Valuable crops, including cotton and sugar, grow well in the soil in the region, because river floods spill **sediment** containing nutrients onto the land. The crops and other goods are bought, sold, and transported up and down the river. Rivers are important for trade around the world.

Amazing Adaptation

Rice plants are adapted to grow in the flooded soil in deltas of large rivers, such as the Yangtze and the Ganges. Submerged leaves trap a thin layer of air on their surface, which they can use to carry out photosynthesis.

People farm rice in flooded fields because the plants grow better here and produce more rice grains, than when grown in dry soils. The layer of water also stops weeds growing.

FRESHWATER RESOURCES

Water is essential for people to drink, to wash themselves and their clothes, and to flush away natural waste. But freshwater resources are in demand for other reasons. Most freshwater resources for people are sourced from freshwater biomes.

Agriculture

Farmers may spray or **irrigate** crops with river or lake water to help them grow, especially in drier regions where there is normally not enough rain to grow food. Freshwater is also needed for livestock to drink, to grow foods that livestock eat, and to process meat and other foods. Shallow water in wetlands and estuaries is trapped in ponds and used to farm fish and shrimp as well.

Industry

Water is used in factories to make products, such as paper, medicines, and drinks, and to cool factory machines so they do not overheat and get damaged. That's why many factories are built near rivers. Water is also an important ingredient in making the concrete people use for buildings. High-pressure water is used for a variety of purposes from mining soft rocks to cutting metals.

Approximately two-thirds of all water used for human activities is used for agriculture.

Energy

Freshwater is widely used to produce electricity in power stations. Many power stations use fuels to heat up water to make steam. This steam spins **turbines** that, in turn, spin the **generators** that make electricity. **Hydroelectric** generating stations produce 20 percent of the world's electricity. They use moving water in rivers and from **reservoirs** instead of burning fuel to spin the turbines.

Recreation

People use freshwater biomes for recreation in many different ways. Tourists visit wetlands and estuaries to see the wildlife. Rivers and streams are a lure for those keen on fishing and also for canoers and rafters. The still waters of lakes, canals, and reservoirs are ideal for boating.

Hydroelectric generating stations use the force of water rushing through pipes to spin electric generators. Dams trap deep water in reservoirs to supply large amounts of rushing water to operate the generators.

Fact Focus: Golf Courses

There are more than 30,000 golf courses worldwide, and all require freshwater, often diverted from biomes, to keep the grass green. The amount of water used on these courses each day could supply the basic water needs of 4.7 billion people.

FRESHWATER THREATS

Freshwater biomes are incredibly useful to us, but sometimes the ways in which we use them can threaten these precious waterways and the plants and animals that live in them.

Pollution

Some rivers are damaged when **pollution**, such as factory waste or oil, runs into them. Substances, such as **pesticides**, that wash off fields or medicines flushed down drains can remain in waterways for years. They can affect food chains when animals eat plants polluted by these substances. In some cases, pollution can make water wildlife sick. In other cases, it can adversely affect animal populations by preventing reproduction.

Disappearing water

People are also destroying areas of freshwater by draining wetlands to create land for building or for crops. This not only reduces space for animals and plants adapted to these habitats, it can also increase flooding on areas of dry land. That's because wetlands play an important role in absorbing water during heavy rains.

Mangrove wetlands in Malaysia have been taken over by shrimp ponds, robbing wildlife of their homes.

Fact Focus: Global Warming

Global warming is the gradual rise in Earth's temperature. In places that are getting hotter, increased evaporation is drying up lakes, wetlands, and rivers. This can have an impact on wildlife. For example, there are fewer opportunities for frogs and toads to breed and lay eggs in these areas.

Blocking rivers

There are approximately 45,000 big dams worldwide. When people build a dam for electricity generation, it floods land upstream and reduces the water flow downstream. Dams are one of the major reasons why big rivers, such as the Rio Grande in the USA and the Ganges in India, are drying up. This is bad news for freshwater animals and plants, partly because it disrupts the natural water levels in the biome where living things are adapted to survive and reproduce.

In some places, people build salmon ladders—water channels up the side of a dam—that fish can use to get to rivers where they breed. However, some are caught by hungry bears on the way.

Fact Focus: Salmon and Bears

Salmon swim inland from the sea to reach rivers where they breed. Dams can stop salmon reaching the rivers they breed in, which means fewer salmon and fewer animals, such as bears that rely on them for food. Bears rely on eating the salmon in autumn to build up fat that helps them survive cold winters.

FRESHWATER FUTURES

Freshwater biomes are incredible places full of fascinating wildlife, yet they are also the source of water that people need. It is vital that we find a balance between **conservation** and water use to ensure that these biomes thrive now and into the future.

Conservation

People are making great efforts in freshwater conservation. In some places, there are freshwater **reserves** to protect the biome and the rare **species** that live there. For example, the Macquarie Marshes wetland in southeastern Australia has been protected since 1900.

Conservation groups protect freshwater biomes by preventing them from being drained to create land, controlling pollution, and clearing sediment away to help the flow of water.

People are making many changes to help freshwater biomes, such as building hydroelectric power dams that control, but do not completely interrupt the flow of water from stream to estuary.

In 2014, the Colombian government set up the protected Inirida wetlands. This was partly to protect **endangered** pink river dolphins in the Orinoco River.

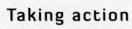

Taking action

We can all help freshwater biomes in different ways. We can use less water by taking shorter showers, using rainwater or water we wash with to flush toilets, or even by eating less meat. Livestock drink a lot, and much water is needed to process meat—it can take 630 gallons (2,385 L) to produce one hamburger! Another way to help is to reduce pollution by not putting oil and harmful chemicals down drains that could end up in rivers. How else could you help?

Local people are working hard to sustain the fishing industry year after year in Tonlé Sap, Cambodia. They control fishing and protect the lakesides from pollution and overdevelopment, which keeps the habitat rich in wildlife.

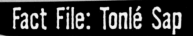

Fact File: Tonlé Sap

Location: Cambodia, Southeast Asia
Size: 6,175 sq. mi. (16,000 km²)
Overview: The abundant fish in the biggest lake in Southeast Asia attract fishing birds, such as cormorants and pelicans, and a fishing industry. Many fishing families live in houseboats on the lake.

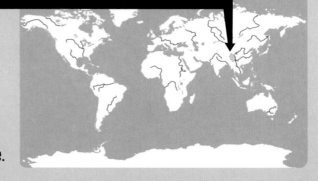

29

GLOSSARY

adapted Special feature or behavior that helps a living thing survive in its habitat

antennae Feelers on an animal's head that touch and sense its habitat

atmosphere Blanket of gases that surround Earth

bacteria Tiny living things that can cause diseases or decompose waste

biome Region of Earth with living things adapted to the typical climate, soils, and other features

breed To have young

calcium A white substance animals can use to build bones, shells, and teeth

climate Typical weather pattern through the year in an area

condense When a gas such as water vapor in the air turns into a liquid (water)

conservation The act of guarding, protecting, or preserving something

dam Wall that stops a river flowing so its water collects in a reservoir

decompose To break down bits of dead plants, animals, and waste into nutrients plants can use to grow

delta Triangular-shaped area of land where a river splits and flows into an ocean

dense Made up of parts crowded together

digest Break down food into nutrients

dilute To make something weaker

endangered When a plant or animal is in danger of dying out

erode The action of water or wind to remove soil, rock, or minerals from one location and deposit it at another location

evaporate When water turns from a liquid into water vapor in the air

exoskeleton A hard covering on the outside of some animal bodies

fin Flat body part on the outside of some water animal bodies that helps them swim

food chain A way of showing the movement of the Sun's energy from one living thing to another

food web A network of related food chains that shows how energy is passed from one living thing to another

generator Machine that produces electricity

gills Body parts used to breathe underwater

glacier Very slow moving river of ice

global warming Rise in average temperature of Earth caused by human activity

habitat Place where an animal or plant typically lives

hydroelectric Electricity made using the power from moving water

irrigate Put water on land to help grow crops

nutrients Substances living things need to live

nymph A young form of an insect that does not change greatly as it grows

oxygen Gas in the air that animals need to breathe.

pesticide Chemical used to kill pest animals

photosynthesis Process by which green plants make sugary food using the energy in sunlight

poles The two opposite points on Earth's surface through which its axis passes; the South Pole and the North Pole

pollution Something that damages water, air or land or makes it harmful to living things

predator Animal that hunts and eats animals

prey Animal eaten by another animal

reserve Area protected to keep living things and landscapes safe from people

reservoir Artificial lake, often behind a dam

rodent Animal with large front teeth for gnawing, such as a mouse or rat

roots Underground parts of a plant that take in water and nutrients from the soil

sediment Small bits of rock, sand, mud or shells that sink to the bottom of water.

species Type of plant or animal

starch Form of energy stored in plants

streamlined Long, thin shape that moves easily through air or water

sulfate A type of salt that occurs widely in everyday life

surface area Total area of the surface of a three-dimensional object

surface tension Property of the surface of water that makes it behave like a thin, elastic sheet

turbine A machine that has a shaft with blades attached and is turned by moving water or air

valley A low area between hills that may have a river running through it

webbed feet Having skin between toes or fingers

FIND OUT MORE

Books

**Endangered Rivers: Investigating Rivers in Crisis
(Endangered Earth)**
Rani Iyer
Captsone Press, 2015

Everglades Research Journal (Ecosystems Research Journal)
Robin Johnson
Crabtree Publishing, 2017

Wetlands Inside Out (Ecosystems Inside Out)
Megan Kopp
Crabtree Publishing, 2015

The Amazon: River in a Rain Forest (Rivers Around the World)
Molly Aloian
Crabtree Publishing, 2010

Websites

Read fascinating freshwater facts and figures at:
www.worldwildlife.org/habitats/wetlands

Check out more facts about this biome at:
www.ucmp.berkeley.edu/exhibits/biomes/freshwater.php

See the water cycle as an animation at:
www.nsf.gov/news/mmg/mmg_disp.jsp?med_id=74613

See a dragonfly adult emerging from the nymph stage at:
www.arkive.org/emperor-dragonfly/anax-imperator/video-09b.html

INDEX